EVANGELISM FOR AMATEURS

Evangelism for Amateurs

Michael Green

Hodder & Stoughton

LONDON SYDNEY AUCKLAND

British Library Cataloguing in Publication Data
A record for this book is available from the British Library

ISBN 0 340 71420 4

Typeset by Hewer Text Composition Services, Edinburgh
Printed and bound in Great Britain

Hodder and Stoughton Ltd
A Division of Hodder Headline PLC
338 Euston Road
London NW1 3BH

Contents

Thank you . . .

- to my humorist friend, Taffy, who did the cartoons for overhead projection;

- to Martin Cavender, Director of Springboard, who uses these overheads with me all over England as we help clergy and lay people to share the gospel with joy – at the request of the Archbishops of Canterbury and York;

- to the Archbishops themselves, who trusted a maverick loose canon;

- to Harold Percy, who said to me when first he saw these cartoons being used in Canada, 'Man, you should put them in a book.'

Harold – and others – here it is! Hope you enjoy it: the Christian life is meant to be enjoyed.

Michael Green

1

Not activism – prayer

The dreaded 'E' word: evangelism! It makes many church people run for cover. The last thing we want to be seen as is mindless enthusiasts passionately committed to pushing our views on other people.

Anyhow, talking about God is embarrassing. It's a very private matter.

What's more, some of us have the lurking suspicion that this Christianity stuff might not be true after all. A bit like Father Christmas – nice for the kids, but make-believe for the grown-ups.

Evangelism is cool

That's how it used to be in a great many churches and denominations. But things have changed. Evangelism has, in the last ten years or so, become almost cool. Cool to talk about, if not to do. Archbishops are commending it. Village churches are discussing it. Lots of new churches

Not activism . . . .

are being started – why, even the Church of England, which has a building in every parish, is starting a new church every week up and down the country . . . some of them in pubs!

There are several reasons for this. For one thing, a lot of churches have no young people, and not many in middle age. So unless something is done, they will be going out of business before long.

But that is not a very worthy motive. Much more Christian is the thought that our Founder, Jesus Christ, was always going around sharing the good news about the difference it makes when God is put into his rightful place in human life. Jesus' final command to his followers was to go and make disciples. How can we claim to follow him if we take not the blindest bit of notice of what he says?

There is another reason. This world is in a mess. Relationships are breaking down, trust is vanishing, violence is on the streets, unbelief everywhere. If ever there was a need for the gospel, surely it is now.

What's more, evangelism is such a joy. Look at the fast-growing churches. There are loads of them in the Two-Thirds world, where the faith is spreading faster than ever before: but there are plenty in our own country too. Isn't it true that members of these churches seem to have a joy and a sense of fulfilment that the rest of us lack? And if you have ever been the last link in the chain of drawing someone to Jesus Christ, you will know that it is the greatest joy in the world.

. . . but prayer

So, yes, evangelism is 'in' these days. But how on earth shall we go about it? Fools rush in where angels fear to tread. And there are quite a lot of fools around! This gives evangelism a bad name. We don't want to alienate our friends by thoughtless enthusiasm, asking them if they are saved, and generally getting up their noses.

God, the evangelist

If we want to draw others to Christ, whether as a church or as individuals, the place to start is prayer. That isn't a cop-out. It is plain common sense. You see, only God can bring about the new start, new birth, conversion – call it what you will – when a person who has been out of touch with God comes into a real live relationship with him, which changes everything. Only God can do that. You and I can't. I remember Billy Graham's answer once to a journalist who was challenging him about the converts in a crusade who fell away. 'Oh,' he said, 'they must have been *my* converts, not God's.'

So if it is only the Lord who can draw people to himself, it stands to reason that the most important thing we can do is not to rush around trying to discover new methods of evangelism, but to pray to God about those we hope to help.

Time and again you will find this is true. When God's people give themselves to sacrificial, intentional prayer for their friends, things happen. Some years ago, in preparation for one of Billy Graham's visits to this country, large numbers of people engaged in Prayer Triplets – three people getting together regularly to pray for three people each of them had on their hearts. The result was that some 18,000 people became Christians in the year's run-up to Graham's visit.

Another marvellous example is provided by the Harvest Ministries in Argentina. They target a city that they want to influence with the gospel. Then they send in fifty couples or individuals, with the brief to find accommodation in different parts of the city, get to know a hundred people reasonably well in the course of the year, and pray for them regularly. The next phase is to send in some gifted evangelists. The friends of the fifty are invited along to these meetings, and many of them become Christians. They are then nurtured in the fifty little groups, which in due course grow into fifty new churches. And prayer is the secret! Let's take that on board, if we intend to get serious about evangelism. It is top priority.

2

Don't think church – think community

The first instinct of Christians who want to evangelise is to ask their friends to church. Now this sometimes works. Worship of God has great power to attract. Moreover, there are people out there who have been longing for a friend to invite them to church. I came across one yesterday, who had been invited along after her husband's death: she came, and kept coming. She has clearly become a deeply committed Christian. Yes, that sometimes happens.

But it doesn't seem that there are lots and lots of people just waiting to be asked to church. During the past couple of generations there has been a big drift away from church. 'I used to go,' they say when you ask them. Or 'My mum used to go.' It is not that they no longer believe in God: the vast majority do believe in God and Jesus. But the church has disappeared from their lives. For some it is because of the horrors they experienced in two world wars. For others it is the grip of television, Sunday sports and shopping. For others it is the awareness that there are

Don't think church . . . think community

so many religions in the world – why should Christianity be the right one? Masses of people today have never even been inside a church, and have no idea what Christianity is all about. Whatever the reason, the fact is undeniable: all the mainstream churches have experienced a loss of members during the past fifty years. Churchgoing is no longer part of the normal way of life of your average punter. So to ask them to church is asking them to make an enormous jump – from where they feel comfortable (home and pub) to where you feel comfortable (church). You are not simply asking them to take Jesus Christ on board, but the whole gamut of clergy, choirs, chants, the lot. It is a different culture. And we have got so used to the church sub-culture that many of us have few, if any, close friends among the non-churchgoing public. We have lost touch with how ordinary people see us. We have wrapped ourselves up in church talk, church meetings and church people. No wonder we find evangelism difficult.

Caring for individuals

We need a radical change of mindset. We must stop concentrating on the concerns of the Church and the Christians, and start from the other end. What would make the Church worth joining for our friends who do not come? What are the needs in their lives which a real faith in Christ could help to meet? Everybody has needs.

- For some, it is loneliness. Wouldn't the companionship of the only person in all history to break the barrier of death be relevant for them?
- Many people today are clear on human origins – evolutionary theory has taken care of that. But they are clueless on human destiny. *What are we for*? The actor Robert Mitchum said, 'I say my lines, kiss the girls, take my money, and run.' Is that all there is to life? What if the supreme purpose of human beings is to know God and enjoy him for ever?
- Others have a low self-image, in this age when image is deemed all-important. This often affects high achievers, too. If we compare ourselves with one another we are bound to get depressed at times. But what if God Almighty thinks us so valuable that he came to this world to find us, and died on the cross in order to bring us back to him? Doesn't that make a difference?

Caring for society

Of course, the Christian gospel does not only relate to individual needs, but to those of society. The first Christians amazed the pagans by the way they looked after sick people whom nobody else would go near, or buried the untouchables who had died from plague. All down history you find Christians taking the initiative in loving care for others. It was the Christians who freed the slaves. It was the Christians who helped found the trade unions.

It was the Christians who fought for decent working conditions for factory workers and prisoners in nine-teenth-century Britain. Today, Christians are in the fore-front of care for AIDS sufferers. When a Christian team had drilled for water in a drought-ravaged Ethiopian village, the Muslim headman said, 'Now I understand the Jesus way.' I think of a Canadian colleague of mine, a gang leader who had been converted, ordained and ran a theological college. He made a great impression for the gospel by struggling with urban planning authorities until they agreed to leave a green playing-field area in the midst of intensive inner-city development, for the sake of the local kids. I think of a doctor's practice, opposed to abortion, which set up an adoption agency for women who wanted to go through with their pregnancies. Yes, if we want to make any impact for the gospel in today's society, we must not think 'church', but think of the concerns and needs of individuals and communities that we want to reach.

3

Not dominated by the clergy – owned by the laity

For centuries the mainline churches seem to have been run by one person, the clergyman or, nowadays, maybe the clergywoman. You might be pardoned for imagining that this is how Christianity has always been. But no. When it first burst on to the scene in the ancient world, Christianity amazed everybody by being the only faith anyone had ever heard of which did not have a special caste of priests to run the show.

It's a funny thing, but the two Greek words from which we get our 'clergy' and 'laity' are both applied in the New Testament to *all* Christians, and not used to differentiate one group from another. The Christian church is a one-class train.

Unfortunately, it doesn't always work out that way. In almost all denominations, from the Roman Catholics to the Plymouth Brethren, you tend to find one official or semi-official person who acts as managing director. Fair enough, if he or she is simply managing things so that everybody can play their proper part. But disastrous if

Not dominated by the clergy . . .

that one person is calling the shots – driving the train if you like – while all the others are merely passengers.

And that is how it is in many churches. Nothing happens without the vicar. He is unquestionably the boss in the church scene, even if he no longer has much of a stage to play on in society at large. And if he is not interested in evangelism, it is very difficult to get anything much going. The answer, of course, lies in teamwork.

The impact of teamwork

God has given gifts to all of us, and he expects us to use them in his service. You can't have a team if someone wants to be a 'one-man band'. To put it another way, we need fewer soloists in the Christian church, and more orchestras. Actually, of course, if the vicar insists on acting like a prima donna and doing everything himself, he is sure to create an equal and opposite reaction: the lay people, so called, will be likely to flex their muscles. And that is just as harmful to the Christian cause as clerical domination.

All the images of the church in the New Testament have this notion of harmonious partnership built into them. We are like a vine, and each of us is a branch. We are like a temple, and each of us is a stone. We are like a body, and each of us is a limb. The Bible could hardly emphasise more strongly that we belong together. We simply cannot afford to set clergy against laity. That is to

23

. . . owned by the laity

hack the vine to pieces. It is to smash the temple. It is to mutilate the body.

Partnership is essential in every aspect of church life, and evangelism is no exception. The vicar may know most about the Bible and preaching, but that does little good if there is nobody in church to hear him. Numbers will only build up if there is real trust between the vicar and the congregation. They have got to know that he is worth hearing before they risk their friends by inviting them to church.

A great army

Equally, it is much easier and more natural for members of the congregation to relate to ordinary non-churchgoing people than it is for the vicar. He or she is regarded with some suspicion these days. It is thought rather odd to be a minister; it is even odd to get too closely involved with one! In any case, one man or woman in leadership of a congregation cannot possibly have as many contacts as the whole congregation can between them. The lay people, if they are fired up, can clearly have a much wider impact than their minister. Potentially, they are a great army, waiting to be mobilised.

It is wonderful when it turns out this way. I often have the privilege of taking teams of people out to share the gospel in different towns. There may well be clergy in the team, but you would be hard put to differentiate them

from the many gifted lay people who come with us. We are all in it together, fully involved in the work of evangelism among old people, teenagers, businessmen, and so on. The most appropriate speaker for the event, whether ordained or lay, gives the talk. Someone else gives a testimony to the difference Christ has made in his or her life. You might have a dramatic sketch by others, as part of the event. Someone else from the team will be needed to handle the sound and the video clips. The point is, we are a team. The partnership in the work, the mutual encouragement, the times of prayer and praise, are such a joy to one and all. It is indeed wonderful when the work of reaching out with the gospel is not dominated by the clergy or by a lay reaction, but is a team effort, clergy and laity together. That is how God intended it to be.

4

Not more activity – more training

Let's pick up from the last chapter. It is all very well insisting that the work of evangelism rightly belongs to the whole congregation, so that when people see an entire church lit up with love for Christ they will want to discover the secret. But how on earth are they to go about it?

That is where a good minister comes in. He will not say, like the man in the picture, 'These are my tools, and nobody else is going to touch them.' On the contrary, he will entrust those evangelistic tools to members of the congregation, and train them in how to use them. Of course, he may not himself have the requisite gifts to do the training. No matter, there are plenty of people who have, and he could lay on a training course and invite one of them to lead it. Alternatively there is a great deal of helpful material in writing or on video. He could make use of that. At all events, training there must be.

Not more activity . . .

Getting the motivation

The most important element in training is motivation. Once you have got the motivation, you are sure to find some way of expressing it. No man goes to training courses before proposing to the lady in his life! However tongue-tied and stuttering he may be, he will communicate wonderfully well, because he is highly motivated. An obvious point, but an important one.

Most people think you need to be a competent speaker and quite well trained in order to help someone else to faith. That is quite untrue. The best evangelists are often the new converts. They have lots of unchurched friends, for one thing. They have never been ruined by a training course, for another! And they have the burning enthusiasm of those who have made the discovery of their lives, and are longing to pass it on.

So lots of work needs to be done on motivation. A good leader will teach about the responsibility we all have to bear witness to Christ by our words as well as by our lives. And that holds good from Monday to Saturday, and not just for a couple of hours on Sunday. Yes, he will teach this: but he will not leave it there.

Sharing the discovery

There is a second area where we could all do with some help, and that is in telling the story of what God has done

. . . more training

for us, without embarrassment and without being pious about it. Each of us has a story to tell: God deals with us all individually. No two stories are identical, and if we don't tell our own story, nobody else can do it for us. It is such a marvellously natural thing to do. No address to prepare, no special occasion to dread. It simply means taking opportunities, as they occur, to make three simple points.

We need to say something about the life we lived when Christ was still 'the stranger of Galilee' to us. Then something about how we came to discover him for ourselves. And then a word about the difference that discovery has made.

It can all be done in a couple of minutes. It has the advantage of being unexpected; people are amazed to hear their friends talking quite naturally about a personal relationship with God. And, best of all, nobody can argue with us! We dread being shot down in debate about God, and so for the most part we prefer to keep quiet. But we can set our fears at rest. Nobody can rubbish our experience. All they can do is say, 'Well, I don't see it that way. I have never had a similar experience.' That immediately leaves open the response, 'There is no earthly reason why you shouldn't discover him for yourself, if you really want to.' You see, people can attack your arguments, but they cannot deny your experience. Knowing that can be such an encouragement in the early days of sharing your faith.

I believe that telling our spiritual story is one of the easiest, most interesting and most effective ways of spreading the good news. If the minister can excite even half his congregation to do that, evangelism will happen all over the area. Because when people hear a friend talking about the joy and fulfilment of this relationship with Christ, it usually makes them curious, even wistful. After that it is not hard to lead them to Christ.

Starting the training

There are two other main ways in which a leader of a church or a Christian group can give training. One is by explaining how we can help someone to appreciate what God has done for us in Christ, and to turn to him in repentance and faith. It is, after all, a sort of spiritual birth, and at any birth it helps if the midwife knows what she is doing! We will look at that in a later chapter.

And what is the other way of training? It is to *take someone with you*, when you are spreading the gospel. Are you going to have a chat with a parishioner in their home? Bring a less experienced colleague with you to listen and learn. Are you speaking at an evangelistic event? Take your less experienced colleague along with you. People learn such a lot in this way. They see you doing it. They realise it is not so difficult or embarrassing after all. They discover that they can do it too. And their freshness and enthusiasm is an additional advantage: it more than makes up for their lack of experience.

Think how the great masters of painting like Rubens and Michelangelo trained their followers. They had them in the studio, watching. Then they got them to mix some of the paint and clean the brushes. Then they allowed them to paint a bit of shadow at the bottom of the picture. Finally they were ready to paint properly themselves. Apprenticeship is the best way of training.

5

Not an occasional raid – consistent congregational life

The picture of the masked raider is not too far from the impression many people have of evangelism. It is a raid. It is an assault on the intelligence or the longsuffering of the hearers. It brings to mind the reaction you have when you open the front door and find the Jehovah's Witnesses outside. Not a happy feeling.

Hit-and-run

Why is this such a common response to evangelism? The answer is not hard to find. It is because this sort of evangelism is unnatural. It is a one-off. It is a hit-and-run type of approach. There is no existing relationship. There is no opportunity for intelligent discussion and thoughtful reflection. The best thing to do is to keep your head down behind the parapet, and before long it will go away, and life will return to normal.

I have a lot of sympathy with those who feel like that.

Not an occasional raid . . .

The crusade meetings, with earnest invitations to leave your seat and be counselled at the front of the meeting by someone you have never seen before and will never see again. The invitation to an obviously evangelistic event in the local church. The little booklet containing Four Spiritual Laws. The earnest atmosphere. Not very enticing, is it? After all, who are these visitors that have come to lead a mission in the town? What are they like at home? Can they be trusted? Are they out for money? And why has the church suddenly interested itself in the likes of me – when I am not interested in the church and have done nothing to deserve their attention? The mind is full of such questions. Understandably so.

Maybe that is part of the reason why evangelism seems so difficult these days. God, or at any rate his church, is out of fashion. Sudden attempts to inject him into the normal flow of life are an unwelcome intrusion. They do not ring true. They are not likely to change our opinions on the deepest things of life. Certainly not in a hurry. Perhaps that is why guest services and crusades on the whole do not reach the great unwashed. They draw in few 'guests' unless some very lively churches are backing the enterprise. Those who do turn up usually already have some sort of link with the church.

It is perhaps encouraging for the would-be evangelist to reflect that these crusades and one-night stands are a comparatively new phenomenon on the Christian scene.

. . . but consistent congregational life

Calling people to respond by coming to the front was a late nineteenth-century idea. Little evangelistic booklets came into fashion in the twentieth. The Christian church throughout the ages survived perfectly well without these methods – which seem to alienate more people than they help these days.

Earn the right to speak

The big draw to Christ and his kingdom has always been the same. It is the life-style of the Christian community. Their thoughtfulness. Their willingness to put themselves out. Their self-sacrifice. Their generosity and joy in God. That is the magnet that draws people to consider Christ and his manifesto for human life. A wise old Scottish evangelist used to say, 'We must earn the right to speak.' He was right.

It makes sense, doesn't it? Nobody is going to believe God is love unless they see something of it reflected in the lives of those who profess to know him. Nobody is going to believe Christ reconciles people unless they see the manifestly reconciled life of those who have nothing else in common but Jesus. Nobody is going to believe Christ is alive and has conquered death unless they see something radically different in the way his followers approach death.

The 'Wow!' factor

Let me give you some examples of the sort of thing I mean:

- I think of a student with severe anorexia nervosa. She was not responding to any of the medical approaches, and was clearly going to die. But the members of the Christian fellowship in her college loved her and stayed with her day and night for weeks on end. Nobody else did that. She was impressed. In due course she was healed. And not surprisingly she soon entrusted her life to the Christ who had made her friends so full of love.

- I think of a city-wide mission on which a team of thirty or so embarked with me in Western Canada. We came from some fifteen different nationalities and widely divergent backgrounds – some from the slums and some born with a silver spoon in their mouths. We had ex-Buddhists, Messianic Jews, ex-Hindus and ex-druggies in the team. And we clearly loved one another very much. Our message of reconciliation with God gained credibility because we were so obviously reconciled with each other through a power not our own. People have a right to expect that, if they are to believe our gospel.

- I think of a funeral in the church I served in Oxford. A colleague took it, and the undertaker described it to me with awe. A young woman in her thirties had died, leaving a husband and two children. It was a Christian family. The children went to the funeral in their party frocks and with bows in their hair. Of course there was deep sorrow in the face of the death of their nearest and dearest. But it was not sorrow that had no hope. It was tinged with the awareness that Christ was the conqueror over death, and they knew him!

Those are the qualities which wing the words of the evangelist. Not a sudden raid, but the steady quality of life among individuals and congregations alike, which makes people wonder, 'What is it these Christians have got?' I call it the 'Wow!' factor. Without it, the masked raider type of evangelism will cut no ice.

6

Not shouting –
bridge-building

It's sad but true that much evangelism gives the impression of being aggressive. For one thing, it is almost always men who do the up-front evangelism. What's more, they are generally extroverts. The approved method is preaching, usually at some length, and without any opportunity for come-back. If you happen to be on the receiving end, it must be very unnerving.

You get invited to a dinner party thrown by some Christians, and you suspect (rightly!) that there are strings attached . . . someone is wanting to convert you. That rather spoils the dessert.

You accept, with considerable caution, an invitation to a big evangelistic meeting, and you suspect (rightly!) that at the end you will be embarrassed by being asked to come forward, put your hand in the air or give your name in for somebody to follow up at a later date.

You allow yourself to be persuaded to attend a 'guest service' at your local church, and you find the milieu unfamiliar, and not necessarily to your liking. A man you

Not shouting . . .

do not know stands out at the front and speaks for some time. The talk may well be weak on reasoning and strong on shouting: lots of heat but not much light. And at the end they want to offer you an evangelistic booklet or to sign you up for an Alpha course. It is all rather distasteful. You determine never to go again.

Many churches which are keen on evangelism use approaches like these. It is true that these evangelical churches are growing fast. But it is also true that they tend to have a revolving door. They must put off as many as they help by tactics such as these. Surely we do not need to bludgeon people into the kingdom of God? There has to be a better way. Mercifully there is.

The personal touch

Just think for a moment. How does God approach us? Does he deafen us with shouts from afar? Does he demand instant response? Does he bombard us with radio messages or telecasts? No, he does none of those things. He woos us rebellious human beings not so much with declarations of truth, but with the beauties of nature, the goodness and generosity of other people, the love of our friends. That is how he seeks to get through to us. And, best of all, he comes in person – yet as one of us, a man among men. He comes alongside. He comes to befriend. And when he has allayed our suspicions and absorbed our hostility, he gently draws us back to the one who makes sense of life, the God who gave it to us.

If God communicates that way, wouldn't we be wise to take a leaf out of his book? We shall get nowhere with people by shouting the gospel at them from the fastness of our churches, or pestering them to come into what is for them alien territory. We need to build bridges, bridges of friendship.

Crossing the drawbridge

I sometimes feel that our churches are like those old castles, with their moat and their high walls. The standard of truth may fly proudly from the flagpole, but the drawbridge is up. So it is hard for anyone from the outside to make their way inside. And equally, it is rare for those inside to reach out. They seem to be two distinct communities, with little in common. We need to get out of the castle, and make friends with the people outside.

There are four obvious places to start. The first is within our own family. They should be our nearest and dearest. It is a great mistake to talk too much about God in the home: they will be highly sceptical. But if we manage to live a reasonably consistent Christian life there, and be loving, considerate and good-humoured, it is sure to make some impression (even though they will not admit it!). We shall have prepared the ground for someone else to do the talking.

Then there are those we work with. That is a natural area to explore, and build bridges of interest ripening into friendship.

Our leisure activities constitute the third area, which it is comparatively easy to develop. Last, but not least, there are the people in our road, our neighbours.

It is important for us as individuals to build a wide circle of acquaintances who can grow into friends. And it is crucial for our churches to develop a fringe of people with whom church members are on good terms, and who come along occasionally to a social or a fun event. That is how trust grows. That gives non-Christians an opportunity to have a good relaxed look at us, individuals and church alike. Gradually they conclude that we are not so odd after all. Gradually they may see that there is something different about us. Gradually they may realise that it is all to do with Jesus. That is how they will be attracted.

Relax and be human

Many of us need to be less intense and earnest. We try too hard. Let's learn to relax and be human – with Jesus just below the surface. The opportunity to share some of our story will come if we are prepared to wait, and pray, and listen. We may even find that when we casually mention some interesting event that the church is putting on, our friend asks if she can come along!

Pressure is the last thing we want to exert. After all, God

. . . but bridge–building

didn't pressurise us, did he? No, love is the language of heaven, and if there is real love in our relationships with those around us, natural opportunities are sure to present themselves. Don't try to pick unripe fruit. God has his time, and if we keep close to him we will often be able to discern it.

So make time for that glass of beer with a neighbour. On with the occasional lunch, or the BBQ in the back yard in the summer. There is no need to talk about God, especially the first time or two that your friend comes over. Just be yourself, and care about him for himself. It is almost, though not quite, true that you can only evangelise friends!

Most important of all, we must ensure that we really build those bridges of friendship honestly, and care for people whether they respond to Christ or not. That's how God goes on loving us. It's an attitude we must mirror.

Don't you love this comment by a young woman to her friend? 'You built a bridge of friendship to me, and in due course Jesus walked across that bridge.'

7

Not condemnation – celebration

One of the many rumours about Christians is that we seem almost to have investments in sin. It is reputed to be the subject we are always on about. I am not sure that we deserve that particular brickbat, but I can see how it came about. After all, Christianity is a rescue religion. It is realistic enough to recognise that every single person in the world does, says and thinks wrong things rather frequently! The Bible is very clear on that. So is the *News of the World*. Very well, what's the problem?

The problem is twofold. For one thing, the word 'sin' makes no sense today. People do not see it in its original meaning as 'missing the mark', failing to be the people we could be. The word is restricted to things like murder and sexual failings. That is a major misunderstanding.

The other problem is even more serious. The idea of guilt only makes sense when you believe in a living, personal God whose love you have rejected and whose commands you have broken. Guilt makes sense then. And you realise that something needs to be done about it. That

Not condemnation . . .

was the situation in Bible days. Indeed, Paul's great letter to the Romans is all about the human predicament *vis-à-vis* God. How can we get right with the God we have affronted?

The climate of the day

But that is not today's question. You find few people going round asking how they can get right with God. The very word 'God' has a wide variety of meanings. It may indicate some far-away impersonal source which started the whole world off. It may mean Gaia, the earth goddess of the New Age. It may mean yourself – recognise your own divinity. The point is that the whole idea of guilt, of moral responsibility to the Creator, is meaningless unless you are convinced that such a Creator exists. Many people are not convinced.

As a result, they may feel bad about something they have done in the past, but they don't feel guilty. 'It wasn't my fault: it was the drugs, or the booze, or the wife . . .' It is *never* my fault. I may have made a mistake, or a miscalculation, or an omission, but I am not guilty. The law courts are about the only place where we use that language any more.

Now if that is the climate of the day, it is no good approaching people along the line of their guilt. We may know very well that they are indeed guilty, as we all are, before a holy God who cannot bear evil of any kind in his presence. But they are not aware of it. And if they are, they won't admit it! So to flog the issue of human sin, wickedness, guilt – call it what you like – is not likely to get through. It may be true, but it doesn't *seem* true to many people today. Condemnation merely gets their hackles up. They give the 'Repent or perish' man at the street corner a wide berth. Don't you? I know I do.

Therefore try another approach.

To do so is not to deny, hide or compromise the truth of the gospel. It is simply to seek a more promising method of engaging the interest and attention of our friend.

Get a life!

We have already noticed some helpful approaches. We could talk about the attractiveness of Jesus, and some aspect of the positive difference he can make to life. That can be very effective.

We could raise the issues of meaning and purpose, which are critical in today's sophisticated Western world, where we have everything to live with and nothing to live for. 'Everyone's got a hungry heart,' observed Bruce Springsteen. Or, to quote Prince Charles, 'There remains deep within the soul (if I dare use that word) a persistent and unconscious anxiety that something is missing, some ingredient that makes life worth living.' Speaking into that anxiety wins a ready hearing these days.

But one of the most effective of all approaches is the path of celebration. After all, didn't Jesus say, 'I have come that you may have life, life in all its fulness'? We Christians somehow seem to give the impression that what we are about is grim duty rather than life: moral rectitude rather than celebration. But in the Gospels God appears as the great party-thrower. He is the King who makes a feast, invites all and sundry, and even sends his servants out to bring in the street people and the homeless. I wonder if you ever think of God like that? You can be sure that your non-Christian friends don't.

So we have got to break the image. We need to show that God is on the side of life and celebration: he invented both. He is concerned to give us joy and fulfilment, not to make life dreary. Very well then, we have to think of ways of bringing this important truth home to people. What about a Christmas banquet, to which we invite all the people who can't ask us back? Or a dinner for doctors, or bus drivers, or police? A sort of 'We appreciate you' dinner? It would amaze people to find the church doing that. A supper for the refuse collectors, maybe? A Valentine's party, perhaps spiced with a piece about human love and the Great Lover who invented it?

The other day I was involved with a whole diocese celebrating in the county showground. There were some 25,000 of them, men, women and children of all types and all ages. The centrepiece was a marvellous Communion service, but there were sideshows, hot dogs, and magnificent exhibitions of dance and music by Christians from

. . . but celebration

Sabah and Sarawak who had come over to lead missions in the diocese. Despite the torrential rain, the impact of a celebration like that was enormous. It speaks volumes about the God in whose honour it is held.

Yes, God is in the celebration business. We'd better catch up with him.

8

Not exhortation – exploration

There is a widespread idea that Christians are always trying to tell people what to do. In other words, Christianity is all about morals, which Christians want to foist on other people. You notice it from time to time when disaster strikes, like the Jamie Bulger murder or the Dunblane killings. And then the politicians rise up in self-righteous condemnation of the Church: 'Why doesn't the Church do something about it?' Christianity, they assume, is exhortation to be good.

All belief systems have some moral code; and so, of course, does Christianity. But Christianity is not a moral code. It is a relationship. And so the important thing is not exhorting people to be good. It is explaining to people who are out of touch with God how they can get right with him, and then live that way.

Not exhortation . . .

Exploring the map

In essence the Christian gospel is very simple. And yet, of course, it is like the ocean, which is shallow enough for a toddler to paddle in, but is so deep that nobody can plumb its depths. Still, it is easy enough to sketch a rough outline of the faith. Why not set out to explore it with your friend, and see if it will stand up?

- Christians maintain that behind whatever evolutionary processes may have helped to shape our world stands the creative intelligence we call God. God is the ultimate source, the sustaining principle and the ultimate goal of the whole universe.
- This supreme being is characterised by holy love. God is utterly opposed to evil in all its forms, and is utterly loving to all his creatures.
- God made human beings as the crown of his creative process. Together male and female represent something distinctive: they are made in his image.
- God intended humankind to be the managing director of his world, subject to God but ordering the world on his behalf with careful stewardship.
- Unfortunately humankind has broken away from that plan of the Creator. We have rejected God's claims on our lives, and we have made an appalling mess of the environment through our rapacity and selfishness. There is something out of kilter, something askew in

. . . exploration

human nature, which shows itself in every one of us. Our human nature is not healthy: it is diseased.

- Yet human rebellion has not alienated God. He still loves us, and takes endless pains to get through to us, even though we have little or no time for him. Beauty speaks of him. So does goodness, love, creativity, communication. He leaves his mark on history, and can readily be discerned both in the immensity and in the incredible detail of the world he has brought into being.

- God took particular trouble to reveal what he is like through one man who, on the whole, trusted and obeyed him. His name was Abraham, and he lived 4,000 years ago. From Abraham's family came the people of Israel, whom God destined to be his special representatives and messengers to the world. The Old Testament is the story of their successes and failures in that role. At least they showed the world that God was indeed the holy, loving Creator, and all other gods were idols, literally 'nothings'. And that prepared for the day when God could begin his rescue operation in earnest.

- He came to this world in person, not giving up his deity, but taking on our humanity as well. In that way he could show that he really understands us, and could reveal to us what he is really like. The life of Jesus achieved both objectives.

- But the most remarkable thing about Jesus' life is that it led inexorably to his death which he, and later his followers, regarded as the most significant death the world had ever seen. They maintained that as he hung in mortal agony on the cross, he burdened himself with the total weight of human wickedness, current, past and future. He took responsibility for all the evil in the world.

- The New Testament writers saw this as crucial in restoring human relationships with God. Christ had blown away the fog of unknowing between us and God; he had broken down the wall of separation; he had cancelled the debt we all owe to the God who is blinding purity. And it is now possible for any man, woman or child to be put right with God and start a lasting relationship with him, knowing that the accusing past has been cleaned up once and for all.

- Christians are no less confident about the resurrection. On the first Easter Day Jesus emerged from the tomb overcoming death, man's last enemy. He was alive for evermore! The consequences of that resurrection are phenomenal. They point to God's purpose for humanity, to know him and enjoy him for ever. What's more, because Jesus is alive, he can be met. Real Christian discipleship begins when we encounter him for ourselves. It continues as we get to know him better and follow him more fully. And it is no individual trip, but a partnership with all other Christians worldwide, whose essential unity transcends all barriers of race and colour.

That is going to call for a lot of exploration, to be sure. But in essence it is not difficult to understand. A child can take it in: brilliant minds may stumble at it. Wouldn't you expect the wisdom of God to be like that? Jesus once rejoiced that his heavenly Father had hidden these things from the 'wise' and had revealed them to 'babes'. You see, the key to it all is the humble, warmhearted response that characterises a little child.

Christianity is not about achieving. It is all about trusting and obeying.

Voyage of discovery

So what any evangelist is trying to do, whether in a large meeting or in an individual conversation, is basically the same. He wants to take people on a voyage of discovery.

His aim is fourfold: 1) to awaken the hearer to the wonder of the Creator God who loves us and died for us; 2) to help him or her to change direction from self-centredness to God; 3) to count the cost of discipleship, which means being willing to go public as a Christian and to give Christ the No. 1 slot in life; 4) and then to take that final step of coming to God in prayer and asking for forgiveness and the new life which the Holy Spirit longs to provide.

That is not the end, of course, but it is the end of the beginning.

Yes, it will need a lot of patient exploration. And there is room for a bit of exhortation as well! We shall want to tell our friend how worthwhile it is to follow Christ, and gently encourage her to take that step of commitment which seems so terrifying before you take it, but so sensible and simple in retrospect.

9

Not crisis – process

When I began getting involved in evangelism some thirty-odd years ago, the received wisdom was to preach for decision then and there. It might be in a student meeting, in a church, in the open air or in a home. We tried to present the good news as attractively and as clearly as we could, and then we challenged the hearers to respond to Christ in repentance and faith. They would then be introduced to some appropriate nurture system.

I have nothing against that approach. It worked then, and it still does – but with a sharply decreasing number of people. In those days, although our society was post-Christian, most people still had a broad understanding of what Christianity taught, even if they did nothing much about it themselves. They might well come to a special service, where an effective preacher could reach them with the gospel. The occasional visit to church like this dulled their mild sense of guilt about not going regularly.

Not crisis . . .

Thirty years ago the evangelist could assume some belief in the God Christians worshipped, some agreed moral standards, some familiarity with the Bible, and some experience of Sunday School and church. This meant that you did not have to teach the basics from scratch, so much as to encourage people to act on them. You did not preach to them a Christ of whom they were ignorant; you tried to help them to respond to the Christ they knew about but did not yet know.

Now all of that has changed.

Not the faintest idea

No longer do people out there have agreed moral standards. What morality they have is generally derived from the soap operas. No longer does the word 'God' make much sense to people. It carries a whole variety of widely different meanings. No longer is the Judaeo-Christian faith a major cultural force in the West. The name of Jesus is simply a swear-word to millions of our people, who know next to nothing about him. The Bible is the book nobody reads. And if you are able to get people together for a serious consideration of Christianity, it is all so fresh to them, so completely unknown, that to ask for an immediate response is ludicrous: they simply would not have the faintest idea of what they were being asked to do.

. . . but process

Your view and mine

There is another and even more formidable problem. When I began preaching there was a commonly agreed understanding that you actually meant something objective when you spoke of good and evil, truth and falsehood. That is no longer the case. 'Good' means 'what I approve of'. You are entitled to your view, as I am entitled to mine. Just don't try to push your values on me, that's all. Values are subjective and man-made. As for truth, there is no such thing. When you insist that something is true, all you mean is that it is your view, and you want to make me agree with you. Truth claims are power games. That is the cry today. If there is no agreed difference between right and wrong, and if you cannot use the concept of truth, then it is very difficult to preach the gospel, and well-nigh impossible to ask anyone to change their whole world-view about truth and morality in the course of a single evening! Difficult, isn't it?

Starting a process

Right, if crisis conversion is not as fashionable as it used to be, what is to take its place? Almost all thoughtful evangelists these days are agreed on the answer. Discovering Christ is not so much a crisis as a process. Not so much jumping from a great height into the arms of the

Saviour but rather starting to walk the journey of life (which we all travel only once) in his company. Not so much a one-off decision by which you are saved for ever, but rather a life-long pilgrimage towards what it means to be fully human.

This is not to abandon the New Testament model. It is simply a matter of realising that there are several biblical models. We have in the past seen St Paul's conversion as the thing to aim for. But what about Peter? When was he converted? It was a much more gradual affair, wasn't it?

In the old days we would have seen believing, belonging and behaving as the three main steps in Christian beginnings, and would have expected them to happen in that order. But today belonging often comes first: people start hanging around Christians, just looking, so to speak. Gradually they get drawn into the fellowship, and the believing part comes slowly and bit by bit. The behaving may well come later still. It is untidy, but then life usually is. And we are certainly seeing just as many solid conversions these days as we did in the past.

Journeying together

The emphasis is, however, very much on inviting people into a process, in the course of which they have an excellent chance of discovering Christ for themselves. People are very unwilling to be *told* anything these days. Authority figures like policemen, politicians and preachers are not highly regarded! No, people have to make their own discoveries. And that is where a twelve- or fifteen-week induction course like Alpha or Emmaus is so valuable. It is based on food – a good dinner, perhaps with wine: a meal like that is always a welcome start, and makes people relaxed and receptive. There is a carefully crafted and attractively presented talk each evening, followed by discussion. No questions are ruled out of order. A different topic about Christian basics is handled each week, so there is a clear sense of progression.

Some members of the group will already be Christians, looking for a refresher course. Some will be new believers. The majority may not know what they are! But in the course of two or three months many good things happen. Enquirers discover that you do not have to throw your brains away in order to be a Christian. They get some of their questions answered. They discover the pull of Christian fellowship before they even know the word. They become clearer about the gospel and what they need to do about it. Nobody pressurises them for an instant decision. They have multiple opportunities during the course to think it over until they are ready to make an informed decision. So yes, there is crisis still, but it takes place within a process. And of course, those who come to faith through this means already have a ready-made nurture group in place to help them to grow.

I recently had the privilege of leading a Mission in the University of Oxford. Instead of asking students to commit themselves to Christ then and there, we encouraged them to sign up for a five-week enquiry course, which we called 'The Mars Hill Tavern'. It consisted of a good dinner in a secular venue, a talk, and discussion round the tables. People stayed at the same table of eight or ten for the whole five weeks, and each table was hosted by a couple of experienced Christians who were able to help people as they wrestled with their questions. A couple of hundred or so signed up during the Mission itself. Within a week or two this number had risen to over 450. Non-Christians were telling their non-Christian friends that they simply must not miss it. And students were finding Christ throughout that course and indeed the following term.

If we are wise, we will go for process in evangelism, rather than crisis!

10

Not tradition – imagination

A very curious thing has happened. Jesus of Nazareth was the most flaming (though peaceful) revolutionary the world has ever seen. The *Magnificat* (Luke 1:46–55), which outlines his life's programme, is a manifesto so radical that it makes the Red Flag seem tame. And yet his followers seem to have become the most conservative of all organisations.

More conservative than the Stock Exchange

You find this in every denomination. The Anglicans love to sing at the end of each psalm, 'As it was in the beginning, is now and ever shall be, world without end, Amen'. That just about sums up the attitude! But it is by no means confined to the Anglicans. The Roman Catholics claim that they do what the Church has always done. The Salvation Army has fossilised ways of doing things that were daringly innovative in the days of

Not tradition . . .

William Booth. The Brethren retain their Sunday evening 'gospel service', once a brilliant innovation, although nowadays hardly anyone turns up who is not already a Christian. Strongly nonconformist branches of Christianity soon develop their own unchangeable ways of doing things. Non-liturgical churches develop the unbreakable sequence which must be followed in their hymn sandwich. 'Oh, I'm afraid we don't do things that way here,' is the silent – or vocal – reaction of many a church when something slightly new is suggested.

The church has become more conservative than the Stock Exchange.

Why should that be? I am far from certain, but I suspect that part of it is our innate dislike of being disrupted by change. Part of it is fear of the unknown. Part of it is being unwilling to risk failure. Part of it is having no living faith of our own, so it is best to make the same noises as our believing forebears did, and hope that nobody will spot how hollow we are. I don't know the full reasons. But I do know that the Church has become one of the most reactionary bodies on earth.

Unfortunately the same is true in evangelism. We are bound by the weight of tradition. Anybody who breaks out of traditional evangelistic paths is either viewed with suspicion, or else thought to have let the side down.

A few decades ago there were only two major forms of evangelism on the market. One was the big evangelistic crusade, led by Billy Graham if you were fortunate enough to get him. The other was personal evangelism,

. . . imagination

as one friend talked to another about the deepest things in life.

Needed: imagination

I am glad to say that nowadays there are many signs of a more imaginative and risk-taking approach.

- Some people are finding bereavement visiting a marvellous way of helping people at one of the most difficult periods in their life. If sensitively handled this can lead to their discovering the Jesus who broke the shackles of death and is alive to accompany us throughout the rest of life and over the dark river of death.
- Christian organisations run holiday houseparties and ventures of different kinds for those at the other end of life, the boys and girls who have their future ahead of them.
- Music is one of the most powerful avenues into people's hearts. It is being used for outreach both in the pop scene and in classical music. Some of the top bands in pop music contain Christians, and this affects the lyrics to which millions listen. I know one man who spends half his time in evangelism and the rest as an opera singer. He finds they blend well together, and naturally many are curious to come and hear him – in both roles.
- Imaginative stuff is taking place on the streets these days. Each year on a given day millions of people will

march for Jesus through capital cities the world over, singing Christ's praises, speaking for him, and encouraging others to trust him for themselves. I recall the amazing scenes a few years ago as I was part of a march like that into London's Hyde Park where a crowd of some 90,000 spent much of the day praising God, praying and dancing with sheer joy. Some of the police were in tears.

- Prisons are tough, but can be a highly fertile ground for the spread of the gospel. Many prisoners know they have hit bottom, and are prepared to trust the Christ who offers a new start, especially if some of their mates are taking the same step. One prison chaplain told me of a revival going on in his prison: he had led more than 800 prisoners to Christ inside two years. Warders too!

- Pubs have become useful places for outreach. After all, the pub is the place where most people like to relax with their friends. It is not difficult for the gospel to get a hearing in the midst of conversations in the pub. Sometimes a singer or a speaker can entrance a whole bar with a brief presentation of the gospel. Just imagine the conversations that follow!

- The Walk of a Thousand Men is a good example. Led by Dan Cozens (a genius at pub evangelism) they take a long walk for several weeks across Ireland or down Offa's Dyke, or through Cornwall, stopping at the pubs along the way. They trust God for their needs, taking only enough money to buy someone else a drink, and

sleeping in churches or halls as they go. The first
Christians must have been rather like that.

- All outreach based on hospitality is attractive. Not
surprising, really, because what is evangelism but
God extending his hospitality to folk who have done
nothing to deserve it? Supper parties, lunches, dinners
in restaurants with a speaker – there are endless
possible variations on the theme of home and food. It
is not hard in such surroundings to talk naturally and
informally about God's good news.

- Sport is another very effective way of spreading the
gospel. Many leading sportsmen and women these
days have become Christians, and are inevitably role
models for their fans. They may well be willing to bear
testimony at appropriate meetings to the difference
Christ has made to them – and their presence is sure
to draw a crowd. When you get a world golfer who has
just won the Open speaking about Jesus on TV, people
sit up and take notice. Sports ministry is not just for the
elite. It is a vehicle at all levels of society. Coaching in
soccer, cricket and basketball, developed particularly in
countries like Kenya, America and Brazil, not to mention the UK, has resulted in many thousands of young
people becoming Christians.

But nothing takes the place of personal caring, the sort of
sacrificial service Jesus displayed in the Gospels. I think of
one family who always keep a room for anyone on the
street who needs a bed. Others show their commitment to

Christ by political action, or by staffing mission hospitals in the back of beyond, or by showing how to improve agriculture in countries ravaged by famine. Others run hospices to enable people to die with dignity, while still others show their love for Christ by welcoming handicapped or orphaned children into their homes from wartorn countries like Rwanda and Bosnia. If only we will refuse to be bound by tradition, but strive to recover the risky innovation of our Founder, we will never lack for imaginative ways of spreading the gospel.

God has given us the precious gift of imagination. Let's use it for him.

11

Not aggression – conviction

'My mother gives me a hard time of it. She is a humanist, and is thoroughly turned off God by evangelists. She thinks they are so big-headed, so sure they are right and everyone else is wrong. They are going to heaven and the great mass of people in the world are going to hell. She can't believe in a God like that.'

That was the substance of a letter I got only this week. It reminds us how unattractive the whole idea of evangelism has become. Indeed the very word is a no-no, despite a worldwide Decade of Evangelism. I had a considerable (though unwelcome) compliment paid me by a publisher to whom I showed this book. He said, 'Evangelism is a downer in bookselling terms. Nevertheless, you may be one of the very few authors who could ride the negative aspects of the word.' Well, I don't for a moment suppose I am. But I try!

Why is it that the whole thing has become so unpopular? Maybe that humanist mum had a point. Whereas most churchpeople seem terrified to say anything about

Not aggression . . .

their faith to others, there are those who are really gripped by it and can't keep quiet. And very often they display tactlessness, narrowness of mind, even rudeness as they try to press their beliefs on you. You get the impression that they think they have got God all sewn up. They allow themselves no doubts. They leave no room for mystery, even in God Almighty! No wonder that attitude stinks.

Aggression is out

No, there is no room for aggression in Christians. Not to anyone. Least of all to those with whom they hope to share the good news of Jesus, who said to his disciples, 'I have not called you servants: I have called you friends.' If we are to have any hope of helping others to discover him, friendship is the way. I trust that has become obvious as this little book progressed, but it bears repetition. There is no excuse for any browbeating, any threatening, any narrowness of mind or arrogant dogmatism in those who are followers of Jesus and want others to find him.

If people see themselves as targets for evangelism, if they realise they have been invited to a supper party only because they are evangelism fodder, is it any wonder that they want nothing to do with the Word and those who bear it? I don't blame them, do you? Yet how often have you seen a preacher whip up the emotions, and build on fear and insecurity while challenging people to commit themselves to Christ? Hell fire still forms part of the

. . . conviction

armoury of some evangelists – forgetting that neither rewards nor punishments will drive us into the arms of Jesus: only his love can accomplish that.

So I hope you will not take anything in this little book as a warrant for aggressiveness. That is not the Christian way. Think how patient the good Lord was with you before you came alive to who he is and what he offers. Then shouldn't we be equally patient with others who are still blind to his appeal? Think back: was it the fear of hell, the longing for heaven, the blazing eyes of the preacher that brought you to a living faith? I guess not. God reserves that privilege for himself, and he does it in a very sensitive way, special for each one of us.

Conviction is vital

Aggression is out. Let's be clear about that, and never allow the impression to arise that our enthusiasm makes us intemperate and brash. But having said that, true conviction is a vital part of Christian outreach. Here is why.

In the first place, we don't give serious attention to someone who is unsure about what he is saying. I'm not going to be attracted to Jesus, or anyone else, if his friends are lukewarm about him. Think of someone who is newly married. They are not lukewarm about their spouse. They are thrilled to bits. They never tire of telling their friends how fortunate they are to have married this wonderful person. In so doing they are not putting others down: they are simply revelling in the love of their partner. Well, it's like that with Jesus. If we have fallen in love with him, it is going to show in our speech, our attitude, our worship, our priorities, our confidence. I saw an advert years ago: 'It sells better in glass.' Quite right. Anything does. Because then you can have a good look at it and decide whether or not you want it for yourself. Very well, our Christian conviction will 'sell' better if our lives are see-through and a credit to Christ.

There's another thing about conviction. It has a strong appeal in a world where many people seem to give little thought to matters of ultimate concern, including their own destiny. Show me a man or woman who knows where they are going and lives accordingly, and it is likely to make a real impact. As a matter of fact, we know it does. For the majority of people who become Christians do so primarily because of the example of some friend or relation whom they have watched carefully for a good long time. That is what has convinced them.

Relationship is central

But there are lots of people who are fully convinced about all sorts of things – and are utterly wrong. Conviction unsupported by good evidence is fanaticism. That is where knowing the scriptures and the historical Jesus comes in. We Christians do not whistle in the wind to keep our spirits up. We base our lives on the unquestionable historical truth of Jesus Christ, the very early records of his life, teaching, death and resurrection, and the worldwide community which those truths brought into being. It is by far the greatest story in the world, and we are part of the ongoing flow of that story. Historically reliable, it makes sense, and transforms character. History, reason and experience unite to give us a proper confidence (not a blind certainty). Christians should remember that they can never prove the truth of their claims. Proof is never appropriate in personal relationships, and Christianity is above all a matter of personal relationship.

No, we cannot prove our case. But we can hold our heads high. It is a very much better case than has ever been made for unbelief. And it is life-changing. Rational conviction carries its own assurance. We do not have to pretend to know answers to all the problems and questions which sceptics throw at us. 'I know whom I have believed,' said the apostle Paul – not *what* I have believed: even so massive a theologian and missionary as St Paul did not claim to know it all. It is right and proper to have a quiet assurance of our relationship with the most wonderful person in the world, who shares and embodies God's nature, gave himself up in love for a lost world, and is alive to share our lives with us. Such conviction, when backed up by a way of life which underlines it, has an enormous appeal. It is the appeal of 'Christ in you, the hope of glory', as the apostle Paul put it. He had seen it making an indelible impression on thousands of lives. 'Always be ready to give anyone a reason for the hope that is in you,' Peter urges his Christian friends, 'yet do it with gentleness and reverence.' That remains good advice for us today.

POSTSCRIPT

Please remember – don't forget!

Let's pull all this together. There are three golden rules to bear in mind if we want to help others to faith.

Christian presence

Jesus did not sit in a library writing a book. You would search for him in vain in the committee rooms. He did not restrict himself to church. No, you would find him in the fields, in the streets, chatting with tax collectors, pharisees, prostitutes, lepers, fishermen – the lot. He was notable for his presence in the market-places, on the streets and in the homes of the people.

The church has, on the whole, not been very strong in following his example. We are much more comfortable when functioning inside the church building. We have become a club for the likeminded, rather than a light out there in the darkness or salt in among the meat that would otherwise go bad. We forget that the church exists for the

Christian presence

community. It is the only society in the world, as Archbishop William Temple observed, which exists for the benefit of those who are not its members. But you would never guess as much!

If you want to help others to faith, you have got to spend time with them. If that means going to fewer church meetings, then so be it. Growing churches often run few organisations in the week, but they wisely train and encourage their members to get out among non-churchgoers and make friends with them.

Naturally, high-profile opportunities to support the community will occur from time to time. When English church leaders marched with the miners to protest against pit closures that would destroy whole communities, that was the church getting involved with society as it should. Both at a personal and an institutional level the church *must* reach out. That means you, too.

Christian proclamation

It is no good being out there if we never say anything. A Christian life-style is absolutely essential, but absolutely inadequate. People might simply get the impression that we are rather nice, and that is certainly not what Christianity is about.

At some time or other we have got to open our mouths. We need gladly and confidently to admit that we are Christians. We need to be willing to share something of

Christian proclamation

the story of our experience of God. We need to be willing to invite our friends to suitable occasions when they can hear the good news. We need to become increasingly competent at helping a friend to discover Christ for himself. Life and lips go together. Neither is a substitute for the other. The Christian gospel really is good news, and we have no need to be embarrassed about it. There is not that much good news around these days. But let's ensure that the gospel really does come across as *good* news – not simply churchgoing or ethics or (worst of all) condemnation of others. There is a living God. He has shown us what he is like, in Jesus Christ. And Jesus has dealt with our accusing past, longs to bring us back to God, and is alive to be our strength, our wisdom, our constant companion. That's not a bad offer, and we should be proud to pass it on in whatever way suits our gifts and personality.

Christian persuasion

Christian presence and proclamation are not enough. There needs to be Christian persuasion as well; those times when you sit alongside a friend and chat over the gospel and its challenge. A time to face questions and difficulties. A time to encourage. A time to say how you felt when you were at that stage, and the difference Christ has made since you took the daunting step of entrusting yourself to him. Is he really there? Would he genuinely

Christian persuasion

accept me? How could I be sure? How exactly could I begin? What next? These are some of the doubts which confront people who are considering whether or not to take the plunge. And it is such a help for them to have a Christian friend around, to bounce such questions off. It is such a privilege to be that friend.

Curiously enough, this matter of Christian persuasion is one of our weakest areas. We may not be so bad on Christian behaviour. We may even be quite good at inviting people to hear the gospel. But not nearly enough is done in conversations over a drink after an evangelistic meal or service to bring matters to a conclusion.

We need to discover how our friend is reacting, and help him or her if we can. To be sure, none of us can bring a friend to Christ. The Lord alone can do that. But I know how grateful I am for the man who showed me the way of salvation, and did not just leave it there but answered some of my doubts and encouraged me to take the step of faith which seemed so terrifying at the time. In retrospect, of course, it was the most important and far-reaching decision of my whole life. But I would never have taken it without the kindly persuasion of that friend.

Presence, proclamation, persuasion. These are the big three, for 'amateurs' who want to be evangelists!